GOAT FARMING

STEP BY STEP GUIDE ON HOW TO RAISE GOAT FOR MEAT

BY PETER DICKSON

Table of Contents

Chapter One: Introduction to goat raising

One good thing about goat is that goat is a versatile animal. Goat can easily adapt to any condition. Today goat is known as a poor man's cow. One good thing about goat raising is that goats can be kept with little expense in a marginal and undulating lands unsuitable for all types of livestock.
After making your decision on the type of goat you want to raise try as much as possible to find a local seller. Buying from your local seller will enable you to get the goats that will be acclimated to your area. Goat that is acclimated to your area will move more easily than goats trucked in from a distance. Try as much as possible to avoid sale barns, since you never know what diseases might lurk there. If you plan to keep your goats in close quarters, try as much as possible to avoid goat with horns. But goats on open range need horns for protection. Also a goat in confinement can easily injure another goat, or even you, by playfully turning its head at the wrong moment. Some goats are polled (born without horns). The rest should have their horn buds cauterized as soon as the buds start to show (usually by two weeks of age).

Furthermore, one good thing about goats is that goats are social creatures and enjoy companionship, try as much as possible to start with at least two. Goats can be, and often are, raised in a manageable herd of about six. Those six may be all does (does are female goat) which you really need if you want milk, kids, or both. One good thing about does is that they produce the softest fiber. Anytime you wish to raise goats for meat, transport, or as pets, wethers (castrated males) make a good choice. A wether is as muscular as a buck (male) but as gentle as a doe. (for seasonal breeding, rather than housing and feeding an intact buck year around) many goat owners find it cheaper and less hassle to use artificial insemination or a stud service.

Furthermore, Milk production requires annual kidding, so if you opt for dairy goats, try as much as possible to prepare to deal with a burgeoning population. Some goat kids are so cute and cuddly, it is very tempting to keep them all. But if you do, your facilities will soon be stretched to the limit and this will make your goats to be unhappy. Kids or surplus adults may be sold to help pay for the herd's upkeep. Prices vary from under $95 for a scrub goat, to several hundred for a registered purebred, to several thousand for a top breeder. One of the highest price ever paid for a goat was $80,000 for an Angora

buck. I pray that you will be so lucky as to have such a goat born in your herd.

Chapter two: Merit of goat raising

Goat raising has a lot of advantage. We are going to look at the various advantage of raising goats. The following are some of the advantage of raising goats.

- One good advantage of raising goat is that goat is a multi-purpose animal producing meat, milk, hide, fibre and manure. In some hilly areas, goats are also used for hauling light loads.

- Another good advantage of goat raising is that goats have very few demands of housing and management. Goats hardly need separate housing and they happily share their homes with their owners or the owner other livestocks.

- Another merit or advantage of raising goats is that goats can be raised by landless agricultural labourers, ladies and children because they can thrive well on variety of leaves, shrubs, bushes, kitchen waste etc.

- Another major advantage of goat raising is that goat raising can be a profitable occupation for a farmer and can also fit well into mixed farming.

- **Another good advantage of goat raising is that goats are really cheaper to maintain, easily available and have a friendly disposition.**

- **Another advantage of goat raising is that goats are capable of adapting to various agro-climatic conditions ranging from arid dry to cold arid to hot humid. Goats can be raised in plains, hilly tracts, sandy zones and at high altitudes.**

- **One good thing about goat raising is that goats are more tolerant to hot climate than any other farm animals.**

- **Also another good advantage of raising goats is that goats suffer from fewer ailments than other large animals.**

- **One good thing you can achieve in raising goats is that goats have got increased digestibility of crude fibre and can produce even on poor quality roughages.**

- **One good thing about goat is that it gives more production per unit of investment.**

- **Also another advantage of goat raising is that goats are smaller in size and have a younger slaughter age.**

- In the area of religion goat meat has no religious taboo and is relished by all sections of society.

- One good thing about goat as a meat is that the meat has less fat and is more in demand.

- Another advantage of raising goats is that goats are known to be foster mother of man, because their milk is considered better for human nutrition than any other species of livestock.

- One good thing about goat is that the milk is cheap, wholesome, easily digestible and nutritious.

- One good thing about goat milk is that the milk is finer than cow milk for example the fats and proteins are present in a finer state and are more easily digestible, especially by children.

- Another good thing about goat milk is that the milk has lesser allergic problems than other species of livestock.

- One good thing about goat milk is that the milk is used as a ayurvedic medicine for person that is suffering from asthma, cough, diabetes etc.

- Another advantage or merit in goat raising is that the milk from Goat has higher buffering qualities and this enhances its value for patients suffering from peptic

ulcers, liver dysfunction, jaundice, biliary disorders and other digestive problems.

- **According to medical report it is said that goat milk has a higher content of B-complex vitamins.**

- **Most of the milk production we consume is from goat milk.**

- **Another advantage of goat raising is that the hide of goat is used for the manufacture of leather products.**

- **Also the hairs from goat are used for the manufacture of rugs and ropes.**

Chapter three: Types of goat Breeds

There are different types of goat breeds. We are going to look at the different types of goat breeds.

1. Pygmy:

One of the goat breed is called Pygmy. This breed is of African origin, it has a small body structure. Today, people are raising pygmy goats for meat but they are basically bred as pets. They can be raised all year round. This particular breed is really okay. Look at the picture below.

2. Kinder:

Another goat breed is called Kinder. These particular breeds are dual-purpose goats bred in US for both milk and meat. This particular breed come in variety of colors and patterns and can be bred anytime in the year. This breed is still okay. See the picture below:

3. Pygora

Another goat breed is called Pygora. This particular breed is a cross breed of Pygmy and Angora raised to produce fine fiber. This breed has three different kinds of fleece categorized according to their characteristics.
This particular breed produces up to 6 pounds of fleece per shear and they can be shorn twice a year. Checkout the picture below:

4. Angora

Another goat breed is called Angora. These breeds are raised for their thick fleece. These particular breeds are medium sized goats having long thick coat also known as mohair. They have a Turkish background. This breed is very okay. Checkout the picture:

5. Tennessee Fainting Goat

This particular breed of goats has various names due to their unique characteristics. One of the most popular ones are fainting or nervous goats named after their genetic imbalance. When shocked or surprised, these goats fall down as their muscles get locked or jammed. Although, they not only provide generous amount of meat but also fleece. Checkout the picture of the breed below:

6. Spanish Meat Goat:

Spanish meat goat is also known as Brush goats. Spanish meat goat was introduced in America by Europeans. These particular breeds are short but have a strong built. These breeds are available in various colors and can be grown in any month of the year. Checkout the picture below:

7. Kiko

Another goat breed is called Kiko. These particular breeds were first raise in New Zealand. Although keeping goats is tricky but Kiko are hassle-free as they can easily be raised even in harsh weather conditions. Kiko breed are heavy producers and that is why is named kiko, Kiko simply mean meat. Kiko breed can also be grown all year. Checkout the picture below of Kiko breed:

8. **Boer Goat:**

Another goat breed is Boer. These particular breeds are South African based goats with long, hanging ears and Roman nose. These particular breeds have white body with colored head and backward curved horns. Although they have a gentle built but are strong and vigorous. Boer goats are mostly breed in September and end in January. Checkout the picture below:

9. Alpine:

Another goat breed is Alpine. This particular breed can easily be found all across US. Also these particular breeds were first originated in the Alps and are also commonly known as "French Alpine." These breeds range from medium to large size and they adapt to their environment very easily. Because of this, raising them domestically is trouble-free. This breed comes in various colors and patterns. Alpines are one of the best for dairy farming as their milk contains an average of 3.5% butterfat.

Furthermore, the downside is that they are seasonal breeders. Checkout the picture below:

10. LaMancha:

Another goat breed is called LaMancha. This breed have a Spanish origin but are easily found in US. LaMancha breed are medium in size and healthy, friendly and sturdy goats. These particular breeds have the best dairy temperament and thus, provide rich dairy produce. LaManch breed milk contains about 4.2% of butterfat but they are also seasonal breeders. These breeds are medium sized goats with small tiny ears that are either gopher ears (sweet rolls) or elf ears (hooked ears). Checkout the picture below:

Chapter four: Goat Housing

In raising of goat, housing or shelter is very important. Goats also need house like other domestic animals for staying at night, security, preventing them from adverse climate, cold, sunlight etc. In some case people used to keep their goats with other domestic animals such as cow, sheep etc. There are some people too who used to keep their goats under trees. In the area of going into a well establish profitable commercial goat raising, you really need to build a suitable house for your goats. In building a house for your goat there are some certain things you need to take into consideration. The following are some of the certain things you need to take into consideration:

- Make sure you select a dry and higher place for making the goat house.

- Try as much as possible to make sure that the selected goat housing area is high enough to keep the goats safe from floods.
- Also try to keep the floor of the house dry always.
- Make sure that there is huge follow of light and air inside the house.
- Try to do the house in such a way that it becomes very suitable for controlling temperature and moisture.
- Try as much as possible to always keep the house free from being damped. To avoid various diseases.
- Try as much as possible not let the rain water enter inside the house.
- Ensure that you make the wall of the house with concrete or by using bamboo poles.
- Make sure you keep enough space inside the house so that the goats can have a place for rest.

Different types of Goat House

Goat housing comes in different types. When you want to start goat raising you can make your goat house by using various designs. Don't forget that specific goat housing design is suitable for specific production purpose. In goat raising there are two major types of housing.

Goat Housing over Ground:

One of the types of goat housing is called goat housing over ground. These particular types of houses are made over the ground. This is the most common house for goats. You can make the floor of this type of goat house with brick and cement or simply with soil. It will be better, if you can spread some dry straw over the floor in this housing system. Try as much as possible to keep the house dry and clean always. Checkout the picture below of Goat house over ground.

Goat Housing over Pole

Another goat housing is called goat housing over pole. These particular types of houses are made with over pole. The floor of the house heights is about 1 to 1.5 meters (3.5 to 5 ft) from the ground. One good thing about this type of house is that it keeps the goat free from damping condition, flood water etc. Bamboo and wood are used to make the pole and floor. One good thing about this house is that is very suitable for goat farming, because it is very easy to clean. And you can easily clean the closet and urine of goat from the house. In this type of housing diseases is also less. Checkout the picture below.

Concrete House

Another type of goat housing is concrete housing. Concrete is used to make this type of goat house and is a little bit expensive. There are a lot of advantages of concrete houses. One of the advantages is that it is very easy to clean the house. Concrete house keep your goats safe from all types of predators. Checkout the picture below.

Goat house

Furthermore, any time you are building house for your goats, try as much as possible to always emphasis on the comfort of your goats. Ensure that your goats are living happily inside their house, and make sure that the house is suitable enough to keep them free and away from adverse weather and also from all types of predators.

Chapter five: Goat Feeding Characteristics

In the area of raising goat feeding is very important. Feeding of the goat will determine the growth of the goat. We are going to look at the characteristics of goat feeding. The following are some of the characteristics of goat feeding.

- One thing about goat is that they are hardy, sure-footed small ruminant. Goats prefer to browse different kind of fodder.

- One good thing about goat raising is that goats can be fed with kitchen wastes like vegetable tops and spent grains of kitchen which can save 30-40 % of feeding cost.

- Another thing about goat is that they don't prefer to eat stale food.

- One thing about goat is that they prefer nibbling, so try to provide feed and fodder at small quantities and at least 3-4 times in a day.

- One of the ways to avoid fodder wastage is that try and keep the fodder on a fodder rack (tatna) or tied and hung in a small bunch.

- Try as much as possible to ensure rotational grazing if you have enough land to spare for grazing.

Chapter six: Goat general Management Tips

We going to look at goat general management . The following are what you really need to know.

- Rearing a healthy good breed is of prime importance for a profitable goat farming.
- Also when there is good quality green fodder and balanced feed this will help to enhance the productivity.

- Try as much as possible to keep the breeding buck separately from doe and kids.
- Try as much as possible to keep the buck @ 1:9 ratio in the farm.
  - Also try to castrate all the male goats which are not selected for breeding at the age of 2-4 weeks.

The following are some of the Points you need to be remembered for breeding:

- Try to get a good breed.

- Try as much as possible to get a healthy and breed able stock.

- **Always try to controlled and monitored breeding.**

Chapter seven: How to easily manage a pregnant doe

There are different ways on how to manage a pregnant doe. The following are the different ways on how to manage them.

1. Be aware that the doe regular oestrus cycle is of 18-20 days.
2. Doe oestrus sign will be noticeable from few hours to 2-3 days.
3. If you want to have an effect breeding, the doe should bred within 6-12 hrs of oestrus.
4. The doe gestation period- 150 + 5 days.
5. Try as much as possible to ensure that no additional feed supplement is required till 3 months of pregnancy.
6. Anytime from fourth month of pregnancy, make sure that there is additional feed for growing foetus and nourishing mother because this is essential, it helps for proper growth of

developing foetus in the womb and increase milk production after kidding.

Chapter eight: How to Care and manage a new born goat

When the new goats are born they need to be properly taken care off. The following are the ways to take care of the newly born goat.

- Try as much to give a special care to the kids for the first 90 days of their age because there is high mortality rate during this age.
- Try to make sure that the doe and kids are kept in healthy, well ventilated, spacious and dry shed.
- Make sure that the kids are protected from extreme weather.
- Try as much as possible not to forget to feed colostrum (first milk) within 72 hrs of birth which has high nutritive value and

antibodies to keep the kids healthy and this will also ensure fast growth for them.

Chapter nine: How to manage goat diseases

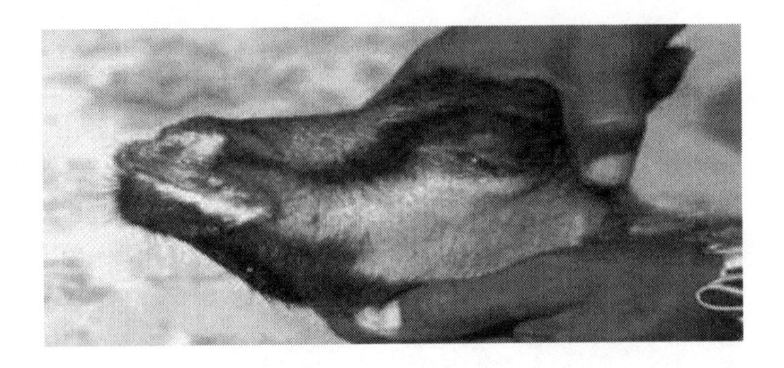

Goats are like any other animal that also face some disease challenge. The following are some of the disease problems goat normal have.

- **There is the one called Mastitis:**

The Mastitis Symptoms: Enlarged hot, painful udder, fever, milk watery with flakes of blood

How to prevent it and treatment: Try to Improve hygiene, and also the application of antibiotics

- **Another one is called Foot rot:**

The Foot rot Symptoms: Lameness, hoof will look as if it is rotten and smell bad. Sign of pain if pressed
How to prevent it and Treatment:

Hoof Trimming, soaking in bath of water with $CuSo_4$.

Another disease is called Brucellosis:
The Brucellosis Symptoms: Abortion in late pregnancy, Retention of placenta and metritis. In bucks- Infertility, orchitis and swollen joints.
How to prevent it and Treatment: Try and Isolate the infected animals, culling of animals.

- Another one is called F.M.D.

The F.M.D symptoms: Fever, lesions on gums, tongue and inner digital spheres stringy salivation.
How to prevention it and Treatment: Vaccination and hygiene, also Isolate the sick animals.

- Another one is called Contagious: Caprine pleuropneumonia

The Contagious symptoms: Diarrhea, Vesicles on the mouth, Nasal discharge, Occular discharge, Fever, highly infectious and fatal

-The last one is called Internal Parasites:

The Internal Parasites symptoms: Loss of weight, reduction in milk yield, diarrhoea, anaemia
Prevention and control: Good quality food and clean water, medication

Chapter ten: Vaccination schedule

The following are the vaccination schedule for goat raising:

Vaccination Schedule

Sno	Disease	Animal	Vaccine	Dose	Immunity	Time of vaccination
1	Foot & Mouth Diseases (FMD)	All cloven footed animals	Polyvalent FMD vaccine	3 ml. S/C	1 Year	February & December
2	Hemorrhagic Septicemia (HS)	Cattle, Buffalo	HS Vaccine	5 ml S/C	6 month & 1 Year	May-June
3	Black Quarter (BQ)	Cattle, Buffalo	BQ Vaccine	5 ml S/C	6 month & 1 Year	May-June
4	Anthrax	All species of animals	Anthrax Spore Vaccine	1 ml S/C	1 Year	May-June
5	Enterotoxemia (ET)	Sheep & Goat	ET Vaccine	5 ml S/C	1 Year	May-June
6	Contagious Caprine Pleuro Pneumonia (CCPP)	Sheep & Goat	IVRI Vaccine	0.2 ml S/C	1 Year	-
7	Peste Des Pettis Ruminants (PPR)	Sheep & Goat	PPR Vaccine	1 ml S/C	3 Year	-
8	Brucella	Female cattle & buffalo Calf age 4-8 months only	Brucella Vaccine	2 ml S/C	1 Year	-
9	Theileriosis	Cattle & calves above 2 months of age	Theileria Vaccine	3 ml S/C	1 Year	-
10	Rabies	All species of animals	Rabies Post Bite Vaccine	1 ml S/C	1 Year	0, 3,7,14,28 & 90 days

Note - Before any vaccination deworming should be compulsory to get better results.

Which you all the best.

HOW TO RAISE GOAT FOR MEAT

BY PETER DICKSON

Made in the USA
Monee, IL
03 February 2024